INSIDE THE NHL

Detroit Red Wings

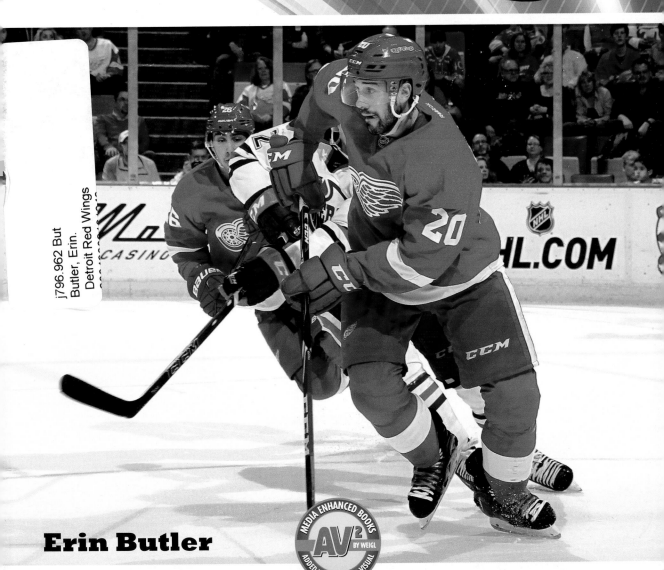

Erin Butler

MEDIA ENHANCED BOOKS
AV2 BY WEIGL
ADDED VALUE · AUDIO VISUAL

www.av2books.com

AV² provides enriched content that supplements and complements this book. Weigl's AV² books strive to create inspired learning and engage young minds in a total learning experience.

Your AV² Media Enhanced books come alive with...

Audio
Listen to sections of the book read aloud.

Key Words
Study vocabulary, and complete a matching word activity.

Go to **www.av2books.com,** and enter this book's unique code.

Video
Watch informative video clips.

Quizzes
Test your knowledge.

BOOK CODE

J893326

Embedded Weblinks
Gain additional information for research.

Slide Show
View images and captions, and prepare a presentation.

AV² by Weigl brings you media enhanced books that support active learning.

Try This!
Complete activities and hands-on experiments.

... and much, much more!

Published by AV² by Weigl
350 5th Avenue, 59th Floor
New York, NY 10118
Websites: www.av2books.com   www.weigl.com

Library of Congress Control Number: 2014952038

ISBN 978-1-4896-3137-4 (hardcover)
ISBN 978-1-4896-3138-1 (single-user eBook)
ISBN 978-1-4896-3139-8 (multi-user eBook)

Printed in the United States of America in Brainerd, Minnesota
1 2 3 4 5 6 7 8 9 0 19 18 17 16 15

032015
WEP050315

Senior Editor Heather Kissock
Art Director Terry Paulhus

Photo Credits
Every reasonable effort has been made to trace ownership and to obtain permission to reprint copyright material. The publishers would be pleased to have any errors or omissions brought to their attention so that they may be corrected in subsequent printings.

Weigl acknowledges Getty Images and iStock as its primary image suppliers for this title.

Detroit Red Wings

CONTENTS

JAN 2016

Introduction

Hailing from the city that has come to be known as "Hockeytown," the Detroit Red Wings are one of the most beloved teams in the National Hockey League (NHL). As a member of the Original Six—the six teams that originally formed the NHL prior to league **expansion**— the Red Wings have had nearly a century to build a storied **franchise** history, including 11 Stanley Cup Championships since joining the league in 1926.

Henrik Zetterberg is one of the Red Wings' hottest current stars.

Red Wings' history is jam-packed with legends that have helped define the entire NHL. Just as they have changed the city of Detroit, they have also changed the way hockey is played and followed around the globe. Despite this strong tradition, the Wings have had their fair share of tragic injuries and championship dry spells. With their eleventh Cup win in 2008, they officially began their climb back to the top of the league.

Gordie Howe, Sid Abel, and Ted Lindsay played for the Wings in their golden age.

Detroit
RED WINGS

Arena Joe Louis Arena

Division Atlantic

Head Coach Mike Babcock

Location Detroit, Michigan

NHL Stanley Cup Titles 1936, 1937, 1943, 1950, 1952, 1954, 1955, 1997, 1998, 2002, 2008

Nicknames The Wings

62
Playoff Appearances

7
Retired Numbers

6
Presidents' Trophy awards

5
Conn Smythe Trophy awards

History

UNLUCKY #42

After their 1955 title, the Red Wings would not win another championship for 42 years.

The Red Wings won seven Stanley Cup titles from 1936 to 1955.

n 1926, the Detroit Cougars began play in the NHL. The team performed poorly and changed its name to the Falcons in 1930. It was not until coach and manager Jack Adams took over in 1927, and the team changed its name again in 1932, that the Red Wings finally took flight. A few years later in 1936, the Wings took home their first Cup after defeating the Toronto Maple Leafs. The next season they became repeat champions by besting the New York Rangers.

From 1936 to 1958, the Wings reached the **playoffs** 22 times, and won seven Stanley Cup titles. This era also saw the introduction of the famous "Production **Line**," which included Gordie Howe, Ted Lindsay, and Sid Abel.

Several key trades are blamed for the long championship dry spell. In fact, the 1970s were considered a lost decade for Detroit hockey. It was not until 1995 that the Wings made it to the Stanley Cup Final again, finally claiming another title in 1997. Since then, they have hoisted the Cup three more times.

In 1997, the Red Wings swept the Philadelphia Flyers in four games to win their first Stanley Cup in 42 years.

The Arena

Joe Louis arena is the third largest in the NHL, with a seating capacity of 20,066.

Until 1979, the Red Wings mostly played in Olympia Stadium. That year, they upgraded and began play in Joe Louis Arena. The arena is named after the Detroit-native boxer, and it has stood as a Detroit landmark since its opening.

"The Joe," as the arena is nicknamed, is known for its bare design, but it has recently been updated to celebrate Red Wings' history. Everywhere in the arena, there are hockey murals, artwork, and photos. There are also championship banners and the retired jerseys of legendary players on display. Walking through the arena is like going on a trip through the history of the Red Wings.

Today, the arena hosts a number of events besides Wings games, including concerts, college hockey games, ice shows, and even the circus. The Red Wings are the main attraction at the arena, however. On September 25, 2014, construction officially began on a new arena, which is scheduled to replace the Joe at the beginning of the 2017 season.

The Red Wings honored Gordie Howe with a statue of the legend at Joe Louis Arena.

Where They Play

British Columbia — 7

Alberta — 4, 3

CANADA

Saskatchewan

Manitoba — 14

Ontario

Washington

Montana

North Dakota

Minnesota — 11

Wisconsin — 8

Oregon

Idaho

South Dakota

Iowa

Illinois

Nevada

Utah

Wyoming

Colorado — 9

Nebraska

Kansas

Missouri — 13

UNITED STATES

6

California — 5, 1

Arizona — 2

New Mexico

Oklahoma

Arkansas

Mississ...

Pacific Ocean

MEXICO

Texas — 10

Louisiana

Gulf of Mexico

PACIFIC DIVISION

1 Anaheim Ducks
2 Arizona Coyotes
3 Calgary Flames
4 Edmonton Oilers

5 Los Angeles Kings
6 San Jose Sharks
7 Vancouver Canucks

CENTRAL DIVISION

8 Chicago Blackhawks
9 Colorado Avalanche
10 Dallas Stars
11 Minnesota Wild

12 Nashville Predators
13 St. Louis Blues
14 Winnipeg Jets

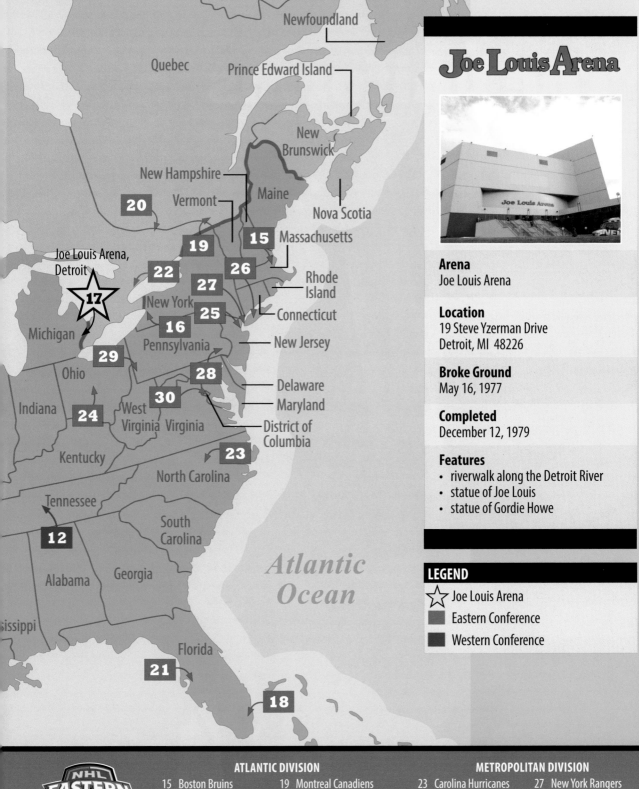

Newfoundland

Quebec

Prince Edward Island

New Brunswick

New Hampshire

20

Vermont

Maine

19

15 Massachusetts

Nova Scotia

Joe Louis Arena, Detroit

22

26

Rhode Island

New York

27

Connecticut

☆ **17**

25

Michigan

16

New Jersey

Pennsylvania

29

28

Delaware

Ohio

Maryland

Indiana

30

24

West Virginia

Virginia

District of Columbia

Kentucky

23

North Carolina

Tennessee

South Carolina

12

Alabama

Georgia

Atlantic Ocean

ississippi

Florida

21

18

Joe Louis Arena

Arena
Joe Louis Arena

Location
19 Steve Yzerman Drive
Detroit, MI 48226

Broke Ground
May 16, 1977

Completed
December 12, 1979

Features
- riverwalk along the Detroit River
- statue of Joe Louis
- statue of Gordie Howe

LEGEND
☆ Joe Louis Arena
■ Eastern Conference
■ Western Conference

NHL EASTERN CONFERENCE ★★★

ATLANTIC DIVISION
15 Boston Bruins
16 Buffalo Sabres
☆ 17 Detroit Red Wings
18 Florida Panthers
19 Montreal Canadiens
20 Ottawa Senators
21 Tampa Bay Lightning
22 Toronto Maple Leafs

METROPOLITAN DIVISION
23 Carolina Hurricanes
24 Columbus Blue Jackets
25 New Jersey Devils
26 New York Islanders
27 New York Rangers
28 Philadelphia Flyers
29 Pittsburgh Penguins
30 Washington Capitals

The Uniforms

The Wings have retired **seven** jersey numbers.

The Red Wings' wheeled design reflects the history of car manufacturing in Detroit, nicknamed the "Motor City."

HOME

AWAY

onsidering the team's long history, the Red Wings uniform has stayed remarkably consistent over the years, as only slight changes have been made. The home jersey is red with a white stripe on each sleeve. The away jersey is white with red sleeves that each have a white stripe. Both jerseys feature the player's name on the back, an addition that took place in the 1970s.

Both jerseys also feature the famous Red Wings crest. As a tribute to former owner James Norris' old team, the Winged Wheelers, the crest is a wheel with wings attached to it. The **logo** can be seen front and center on the jersey, and its design highlights the team colors of red and white.

When the Wings make the playoffs, other Detroit sports teams support them. The neighboring Detroit Lions of the National Football League (NFL) dressed their mascot in a Red Wings jersey.

Helmets and Face Masks

The Red Wings are one of a handful of NHL teams to have their **TEAM NAME** appear on their helmets.

Team helmets are red, with the words "Red Wings" written in a styled font across the top.

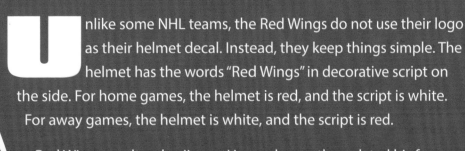

Unlike some NHL teams, the Red Wings do not use their logo as their helmet decal. Instead, they keep things simple. The helmet has the words "Red Wings" in decorative script on the side. For home games, the helmet is red, and the script is white. For away games, the helmet is white, and the script is red.

Red Wings goaltender Jimmy Howard recently updated his face mask with a design that is both personal and team related. The helmet features his number, 35, on the chin, in addition to the letter "D" in old-fashioned script. This is the team's secondary logo. He also has added feathers to represent wings. Goaltenders for the Wings have been known to have fun with their masks. One goaltender even featured the cartoon character Peter Griffin of Family Guy on his mask in 2013.

Jimmy Howard, or "Howie," pays respect to team roots, with the word Hockeytown written across the back of his helmet.

The Coaches

4 Red Wings coaches have won the Jack Adams Award for coach of the year four times.

Unless they are playing in an outdoor game, most NHL coaches are seen on the bench wearing suits and ties.

The Red Wings have employed some of the most legendary coaches in NHL history. They have a habit of finding coaches and sticking with them for a long time. As the team has continued to grow into the powerhouse it is today, coaches have shifted their tactics from being heavy on offense to finding a balance between offense and defense. This has proven to be a winning combination.

JACK ADAMS Jack Adams began his career as a player in the NHL, but he is better known for his coaching. As head coach and general manager for the young Red Wings, he quickly established a tradition of excellence. He made such an impact with the Wings that the NHL's coach of the year award was named in his honor.

SCOTTY BOWMAN With nine Stanley Cup wins as a head coach, Scotty Bowman is a record-setting legend. Bowman is known for his intelligence and his amazing ability to tap into each player's best talents. He coached for a number of NHL teams, and he led the Red Wings to their first Stanley Cup in 42 years in 1997.

MIKE BABCOCK As the current coach for the Red Wings, Mike Babcock has been with the team for more than nine seasons. He has held the Wings to a high standard, leading them to two Presidents' Trophy awards for most points in a season during his time as coach. Babcock also coached Team Canada to two gold medals in both the 2010 and 2014 Olympics.

Fans and
the Internet

Fans come out in large numbers to support their Red Wings, filling up the Joe nightly since 1979.

Red Wings fans are a fiercely dedicated group, visiting and maintaining fan websites, such as Winging It in Motown, Octopus Thrower, and DetroitHockey.net. They connect with each other from all over the globe on LetsGoWings.com. Many fans take pride in supporting the Wings' charitable programs.

The best-known tradition among Wings fans is the throwing of an octopus onto the ice during the playoffs. This tradition began in 1952 when eight playoff wins were needed by a team to win the Cup. The eight arms of the octopus represent the eight wins. The tradition has continued into the present, even though some arena administrators have complained. One year, fans threw an octopus that weighed 50 pounds.

Signs
of a fan

#1 Red Wings fans are vocal in their fierce rivalry with the Colorado Avalanche, often chanting loudly directly over the Avs' bench.

#2 The Red Wings Kids Club gives young people access to exclusive events such as the annual ice skating party at Joe Louis Arena.

Legends of the Past

Many great players have suited up for the Red Wings. A few of them have become icons of the team and the city it represents.

Steve Yzerman

When Steve Yzerman joined the Red Wings in 1983, they were a struggling team looking for someone to get them back on track. Yzerman was that person. Immediately setting records for the team as a **rookie**, Yzerman quickly proved to be a leader, and he was named captain. He would go on to play his entire career with Detroit, becoming the longest-serving captain in the NHL. With his skilled playmaking and knack for putting the puck in the net, Yzerman helped the Wings break a 42-year dry spell to win three Stanley Cup titles.

Position: Center
NHL Seasons: 22 (1983–2006)
Born: May 9, 1965, in Cranbrook, British Columbia, Canada

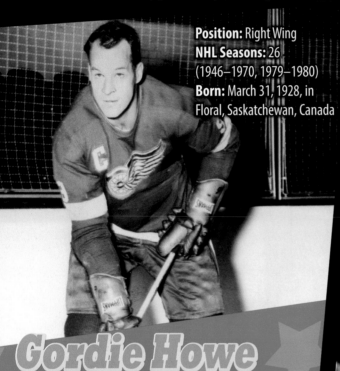

Position: Right Wing
NHL Seasons: 26 (1946–1970, 1979–1980)
Born: March 31, 1928, in Floral, Saskatchewan, Canada

Gordie Howe

Nicknamed "Mr. Hockey," Gordie Howe is a true legend in the hockey world. Howe played his first NHL season in 1946–1947. Though he was noted for his size and skill as a player who could play either right-handed or left-handed, he did not make an immediate impact. His game quickly improved, and by the time he was put on a line with Sid Abel and Ted Lindsay to form the "Production Line" in 1948, he was on his way to greatness. Howe would go on to play through the 1970s, winning four Stanley Cup titles and scoring 975 career goals.

Nicklas Lidstrom

Nicklas Lidstrom spent his entire career with the Red Wings, and he joined Steve Yzerman in bringing the team into a new era of success. As one of the league's top defensemen, he won the James Norris Memorial Trophy for best defenseman an astonishing seven times. During his career with the Wings, he took home four Stanley Cup titles. Lidstrom was the first European-born NHL player to win the Conn Smythe Trophy as the Most Valuable Player (MVP) of the playoffs, and the first European-born captain to win the Stanley Cup.

Position: Defenseman
NHL Seasons: 20 (1991–2012)
Born: April 28, 1970, in Vasteras, Sweden

Ted Lindsay

As a member of the famed "Production Line," Ted Lindsay was a star forward for the Red Wings in what many fans consider the team's golden age. While surrounded by other stars, Lindsay's offensive play touched new heights as he led the league in points in the 1949–1950 season. Lindsay was known for his tough attitude and for his willingness to fight for players' rights. Along with other NHL players, he formed the NHL Players' Association in 1967. Although Lindsay was traded to the Blackhawks, he came back to finish his career with the Red Wings in the 1964–1965 season.

Position: Left Wing
NHL Seasons: 17 (1944–1965)
Born: July 29, 1925, in Renfrew, Ontario, Canada

Stars of Today

Today's Red Wings team is made up of many young, talented players who have proven that they are among the best in the league.

Henrik Zetterberg

Henrik Zetterberg is a powerful goal-scoring force for the Red Wings, the team he has played for since joining the NHL in 2002. With good instincts, a strong **slap shot**, and a cool head under pressure, Zetterberg has been a cornerstone for the team, earning him the position of captain. His impressive goal-scoring ability helped the Red Wings to a Stanley Cup title in 2008. Zetterberg is also a member of the Triple Gold Club, meaning he has won a Stanley Cup, a World Championship gold medal, and an Olympic gold medal.

Position: Left Wing
NHL Seasons: 12 (2001–Present)
Born: October 9, 1980, in Njurunda, Sweden

Pavel Datsyuk

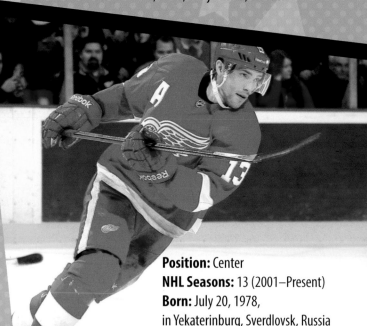

Pavel Datsyuk is a key member of the Red Wings' offensive attack. He has consistently led his team in points, due in part to his patience and stickhandling skills. His game has only improved over the years. In tribute to his all-around skills, Datsyuk has won the Frank J. Selke Trophy as best defensive forward twice. Even more impressive is his sportsmanship, as he won the Lady Byng Memorial Trophy for sportsmanship four years in a row, becoming only the second NHL player to do so.

Position: Center
NHL Seasons: 13 (2001–Present)
Born: July 20, 1978, in Yekaterinburg, Sverdlovsk, Russia

Jimmy Howard

Goaltender Jimmy Howard is one of the Red Wings' hardest-working and most dependable players. In the net, he is known for his impressive stamina and a level of flexibility that allows him to make spectacular saves. In 2012, he became the first Red Wing to tally 35 or more wins in each of his first three seasons. Howard made the NHL **All-Star** Game in 2012, and the following season he led the league in **shutouts**. Howard's incredible determination sets the tone for the hardworking Red Wings.

Position: Goaltender
NHL Seasons: 8 (2005–Present)
Born: March 26, 1984, in Syracuse, New York, United States

Niklas Kronwall

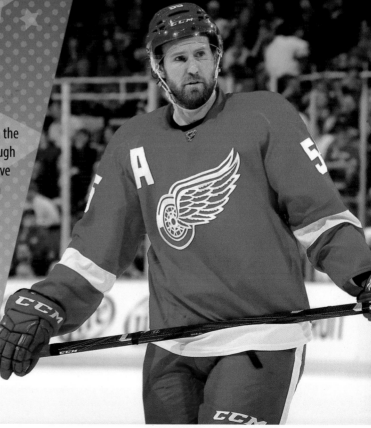

Nicklas Kronwall is key defensive presence in the Red Wings' strong all-around lineup. Although he is a defenseman, he also showcases great offensive skills, leading to his unusually high point totals for a defender. Like teammate Henrik Zetterberg, he is a member of the Triple Gold Club with a Stanley Cup, World Championship gold, and Olympic gold under his belt. In addition to his hockey skills, Kronwall is great with fans. He even serves as president for the Detroit Red Wings Kids Club.

Position: Defenseman
NHL Seasons: 11 (2003–Present)
Born: January 12, 1981, in Stockholm, Sweden

All-Time Records

23
Home Wins in a Row
In 2012, the Red Wings won an incredible 23 straight home games, setting a record that no team is likely to break soon.

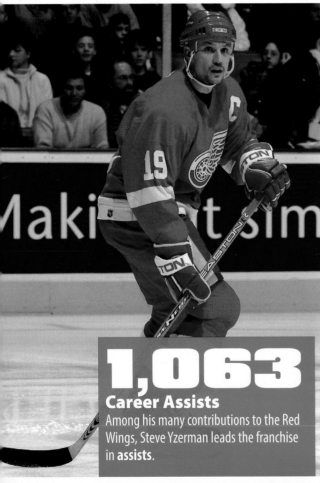

1,063
Career Assists
Among his many contributions to the Red Wings, Steve Yzerman leads the franchise in **assists**.

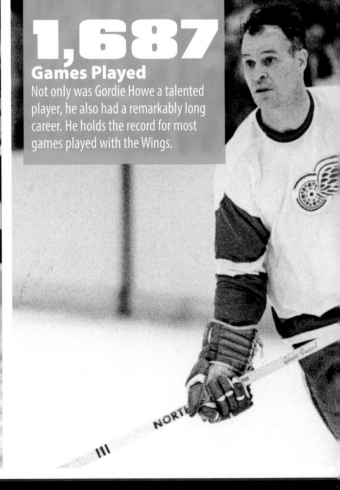

1,687
Games Played
Not only was Gordie Howe a talented player, he also had a remarkably long career. He holds the record for most games played with the Wings.

.56
Goals Per Game
Mickey Redmond scored 0.56 goals per game for the Red Wings from 1971 to 1976, setting the record for highest average of goals per game.

351
Wins as Goaltender
Terry Sawchuk played on and off for Detroit from 1949 through 1969 and racked up the most goaltender wins for the team during that time.

Timeline

Throughout the team's history, the Red Wings have had many memorable events that have become defining moments for the team and its fans.

1926
Detroit is awarded an NHL franchise. The team would play as the Cougars, then the Falcons, and finally the Red Wings.

1936
Led by coach Jack Adams, the Red Wings win their first Stanley Cup championship when they beat the Toronto Maple Leafs.

1910 1920 1930 1940 1950 1960

In March 24, 1936, the Red Wings win the longest game in NHL history against the Montreal Maroons. The game goes into an astonishing six overtime periods.

1952
An octopus is thrown on the ice at the Red Wings' arena during the playoffs, starting a tradition that continues to this day.

1997

The Red Wings, led by captain Steve Yzerman, sweep the Philadelphia Flyers to win their first Stanley Cup title in 42 years.

In 1982, the Red Wings are sold to Mike and Marian Ilitch. The new ownership revitalizes the team and returns the Wings back to their former glory.

The Future

With their long history of excellence and their dedicated players, fans, and administrators, the Red Wings are at the heart of the NHL and its history. Although it has been a few years since they have won a championship, the Red Wings consistently play with heart and skill, a combination that has earned the franchise countless victories for decades.

| 1970 | 1980 | 1990 | 2000 | 2010 | 2020 |

1979

The Red Wings play their first game at Joe Louis Arena. The new arena, known as "The Joe," has 20,066 seats.

2014

The owners of the Red Wings, Mike and Marian Ilitch, announce their plans to build a new arena for the team, which will open in 2017.

Write a Biography

Life Story

A person's life story can be the subject of a book. This kind of book is called a biography. Biographies often describe the lives of people who have achieved great success. These people may be alive today, or they may have lived many years ago. Reading a biography can help you learn more about a great person.

Get the Facts

Use this book, and research in the library and on the internet, to find out more about your favorite Red Wing. Learn as much about this player as you can. What position does he play? What are his statistics in important categories? Has he set any records? Also, be sure to write down key events in the person's life. What was his childhood like? What has he accomplished off the field? Is there anything else that makes this person special or unusual?

Use the Concept Web

A concept web is a useful research tool. Read the questions in the concept web on the following page. Answer the questions in your notebook. Your answers will help you write a biography.

Concept Web

Adulthood
- Where does this individual currently reside?
- Does he or she have a family?

Your Opinion
- What did you learn from the books you read in your research?
- Would you suggest these books to others?
- Was anything missing from these books?

Childhood
- Where and when was this person born?
- Describe his or her parents, siblings, and friends.
- Did this person grow up in unusual circumstances?

Accomplishments off the Field
- What is this person's life's work?
- Has he or she received awards or recognition for accomplishments?
- How have this person's accomplishments served others?

Write a Biography

Help and Obstacles
- Did this individual have a positive attitude?
- Did he or she receive help from others?
- Did this person have a mentor?
- Did this person face any hardships?
- If so, how were the hardships overcome?

Accomplishments on the Field
- What records does this person hold?
- What key games and plays have defined his career?
- What are his stats in categories important to his position?

Work and Preparation
- What was this person's education?
- What was his or her work experience?
- How does this person work?
- What is the process he or she uses?

Trivia Time

Take this quiz to test your knowledge of the Red Wings. The answers are printed upside down under each question.

1 The Red Wings are part of a group of how many original NHL teams that still play today?

A. Six

2 What was the line made up of Gordie Howe, Sid Abel, and Ted Lindsay, called?

A. The Production Line

3 Which Red Wings head coach had a coaching award named for him?

A. Jack Adams

4 What is the name of the home arena where the Detroit Red Wings currently play?

A. Joe Louis Arena

5 Who is the current head coach for the Wings?

A. Mike Babcock

6 How many times have the Red Wings won the Stanley Cup?

A. 11

7 What were the Red Wings called before they were given their current name?

A. The Cougars and the Falcons

8 What are the Red Wings' team colors?

A. Red and white

9 Which head coach led the Wings to their first championship title in 42 years?

A. Scotty Bowman

Key Words

All-Star: a game made for the best-ranked players in the NHL that happens mid-season. A player can be named an All-Star and then be sent to play in this game.

assists: a statistic that is attributed to up to two players of the scoring team who shoot, pass, or deflect the puck toward the scoring teammate

expansion: expansion in the NHL is marked by the addition of a new franchise. The league last expanded in 2000 when the Columbus Blue Jackets and Minnesota Wild joined the NHL.

franchise: a team that is a member of a professional sports league

line: forwards who play in a group, or "shift," during a game

logo: a symbol that stands for a team or organization

playoffs: a series of games that occur after regular season play

rookie: a player age 26 or younger who has played no more than 25 games in a previous season, nor six or more games in two previous seasons

shutouts: games in which the losing team is blocked from making any goals

slap shot: a hard shot made by raising the stick about waist high before striking the puck with a sharp slapping motion

Index

Log on to www.av2books.com

AV² by Weigl brings you media enhanced books that support active learning. Go to www.av2books.com, and enter the special code found on page 2 of this book. You will gain access to enriched and enhanced content that supplements and complements this book. Content includes video, audio, weblinks, quizzes, a slide show, and activities.

AV² Online Navigation

Book Pages
AV² pages directly correspond to pages in the book.

Audio
Listen to sections of the book read aloud.

Video
Watch informative video clips.

Embedded Weblinks
Gain additional information for research.

Try This!
Complete activities and hands-on experiments.

Key Words
Study vocabulary, and complete a matching word activity.

Quizzes
Test your knowledge.

Slide Show
View images and captions, and prepare a presentation.

AV² was built to bridge the gap between print and digital. We encourage you to tell us what you like and what you want to see in the future.

Sign up to be an AV² Ambassador at www.av2books.com/ambassador.